THE SIMPLE WISDOM OF
POPE FRANCIS

THE FULLNESS
OF LIFE

D0249976

Libreria Editrice Vaticana

United States Conference of Catholic Bishops
Washington, DC

First printing, July 2014

ISBN 978-1-60137-473-8

CONTENTS

INTRODUCTION

You have in your possession one of the volumes of *The Simple Wisdom of Pope Francis* series, the first compilation of Pope Francis's teachings.

Immediately after his election on March 13th 2013, the world turned their eyes to the new Successor of Peter to notice Pope Francis's simple ways, humbleness, and his love for the poor and the sick.

This collection captures the wisdom of Pope Francis during his general audiences, which are regularly held on Wednesdays when the pope is in Rome. The general audiences give pilgrims and visitors a chance to "see the pope" and receive the Papal Blessing, or Apostolic Blessing, from the successor of the Apostle Peter. General audiences with the pope are spoken mainly in Italian, but also in English, French, Spanish, or other languages depending on the groups visiting. They consist of short, scripturally-based teachings in which the pope instructs the faithful across the world.

It is our prayer that the teachings of the Holy Father within this series will be a source of hope and help in embracing the grace of faith a little more each day.

LORD, INCREASE OUR FAITH!

OCTOBER 6, 2013

ST. PETER'S SQUARE

Dear Brothers and Sisters, good morning!

First of all, I want to give thanks to God for the day I spent in Assisi, the day before yesterday. Just think, it was my first visit to Assisi and it was a great gift to make this pilgrimage on the Feast of St. Francis. I thank the people of Assisi for their warm welcome: thank you very much!

Today, the Reading from the Gospel begins like this: "The apostles said to the Lord, 'Increase our faith!'" (Lk 17:5). It seems that we can all make this our invocation, especially during this Year of Faith. Let us too, like the Apostles, say to the Lord: "Increase our faith!" Yes, Lord, our faith is small, our faith is weak and fragile, but we offer it to you as it is, so that you can make it grow.

Would it be good to say this all together? Shall we repeat together: "Lord, increase our faith!"? Shall we? Everyone: Lord, increase our faith! Lord, increase our faith! Lord, increase our faith! Make it grow!

And how does the Lord answer us? He responds: "If you had faith as a grain of mustard seed, you could say to this sycamine tree, 'Be rooted up, and be planted in the sea,' and it would obey you" (v. 6). A mustard seed is tiny, yet Jesus says that faith this size, small but true and sincere, suffices to achieve what is humanly impossible, unthinkable. And it is true! We all know people who are simple, humble, but whose faith is so strong it can move mountains! Let us think, for example, of some mothers and fathers who face very difficult situations; or of some sick, and even gravely ill, people who transmit serenity to those who come to visit them. These people, because of their faith, do not boast about what they do, rather, as Jesus asks in the Gospel, they say: "'We are unworthy servants; we have only done what was our duty" (Lk 17:10). How many people among us have such strong, humble faith, and what good they do!

> **A mustard seed is tiny, yet Jesus says that faith this size, small but true and sincere, suffices to achieve what is humanly impossible, unthinkable.**

In this month of October, that is dedicated in a special way to missions, let us bear in mind the many missionaries, men and women, who in order to bring the Gospel have overcome obstacles of every kind, they have truly given their lives. As St. Paul says to Timothy: "Do not be ashamed then of testifying to our Lord, nor of me his prisoner, but take your share of suffering for the gospel in the power of God" (2 Tim 1:8). This, however, is for us all; each one of us in our own daily lives can testify to Christ by the power of God, the power of faith. The faith we have is miniscule, but it is strong! With this power to testify to Jesus Christ, to be Christians with our life, with our witness!

And how do we draw from this strength? We draw it from God in prayer. Prayer is the breath of faith: in a relationship of trust, in a relationship of love, dialogue cannot be left out, and prayer is the dialogue of the soul with God. October is also the month of the Rosary, and on this first Sunday it is tradition to recite the Prayer to Our Lady of Pompeii, the Blessed Virgin Mary of the Most Holy Rosary. Let us join spiritually together in this act of trust in our Mother, and let us receive from her hands the crown of the Rosary: The Rosary is a school of prayer, the Rosary is a school of faith!

Dear brothers and sisters, yesterday in Modena, Rolando Rivi was proclaimed blessed. He was a seminarian of that land, Emilia, who was killed in 1945 when he was fourteen years old out of hatred for his faith. He was guilty only of wearing a cassock during a period when violence was unleashed against the clergy for having raised their voice in the name of God to condemn massacres that immediately followed the war. But faith in Jesus conquers the spirit of the world! Let us give thanks to God for this young martyr and for his heroic witness to the Gospel. And how many fourteen-year-olds, today, keep their eyes fixed on this example: a courageous young person who knew where he had to go, who knew the love of Jesus in his heart and gave his life for him. A beautiful example for young people!

I would like to remember together with you the people who lost their lives in Lampedusa this past Thursday. Let us all pray in silence for these our brothers and sisters: women, men, children . . . Allow our hearts to weep. Let us pray in silence.

I wish everyone a good Sunday. Have a good lunch and goodbye!

I BELIEVE IN ONE, HOLY, CATHOLIC CHURCH

OCTOBER 9, 2013

ST. PETER'S SQUARE

Dear Brothers and Sisters, good morning!

You were very courageous to come out today in this bad weather: my compliments!

"I believe in one, holy, catholic . . . Church." Today we pause to reflect on this mark of the Church: we say she is catholic, it is the Year of Catholicity. First of all: what does catholic mean? It comes from the Greek *"kath'olon"* which means "according to the whole," the totality. In what sense does this totality apply to the Church? In what sense do we say the Church is catholic? I would say there are three basic meanings.

1. The first. The Church is catholic because she is the space, the home in which *the faith* is proclaimed to us *in its entirety*, in which the salvation brought to us by Christ is offered to everyone. The Church enables us to encounter the mercy of God which transforms us, for in her Jesus Christ is present who has given her the true confession of faith, the fullness of the sacramental life and the authenticity of the ordained ministry. In the Church each one of us finds what is needed to believe, to live as Christians, to become holy and to journey to every place and through every age.

To give an example, we can say that it is like family life. In the family, everything that enables us to grow, to mature and to live is given to each of us. We cannot grow up by ourselves, we cannot journey on our own, in isolation; rather, we journey and grow in a community, in a family. And so it is in the Church! In the Church we can listen to the Word of God with the assurance that it is the message that the Lord has given us; in the Church we can encounter the Lord in the Sacraments, which are the open windows through which the light of God is given to us, streams from which we can draw God's very life; in the Church we learn to live in the communion and love that comes from God. Each one of us can ask himself or herself today: how do I live in the Church? When I go to church, is it as though I were at the stadium, at a football match? Is it as though I were at the cinema? No, it is something else. How do I go to church? How do I receive the gifts that the Church offers me to grow and mature as a Christian? Do I participate in the life of the community or do I go to church and withdraw into my own problems, isolating myself from others? In this first sense, the Church is catholic because she is everyone's home. Everyone is a child of the Church and in her all find their home.

2. A second meaning: the Church is catholic because she is *universal*, she is spread abroad through every part of the world and she proclaims the Gospel to every man and to every woman. The

....

In the Church each one of us finds what is needed to believe, to live as Christians, to become holy and to journey to every place and through every age.

Church is not a group of elite; she does not only concern the few. The Church has no limits; she is sent to the totality of people, to the totality of the human race. And the one Church is present even in her smallest parts. Everyone can say: in my parish the Catholic Church is present, since it too is part of the universal Church, since it too contains the fullness of Christ's gifts: the faith, the sacraments, the [ordained] ministry; it is in communion with the bishop, with the Pope and it is open to everyone without distinction. The Church does not rest solely beneath the shadow of our steeple; rather, she embraces a vast number of peoples and nations who profess the same faith, are nourished by the same Eucharist, and are served by the same pastors. To feel that we are in communion with the whole Church, with all of the Catholic communities of the world great and small! This is beautiful! And then, to feel we are all on mission, great and small communities alike, that we all must open our doors and go out for the sake of the Gospel. Let us ask ourselves then: what do I do in order to communicate to others the joy of encountering the Lord, the joy of belonging to the Church? Proclaiming and bearing witness to the faith is not the work of the few; it also concerns me, you, each one of us!

3. A third and final thought: the Church is catholic, because she is the "home of harmony" where *unity and diversity* know how to merge in order to become a great source of wealth. Let us think about the image of a symphony, which implies accord, harmony, various instruments playing together. Each one preserves its own unmistakable timbre and the sounds characteristic of each blend together around a common theme. Then there is the one who directs it, the conductor, and as the symphony is performed all play together in "harmony," but the timbre of each individual instrument is never eliminated; indeed, the uniqueness of each is greatly enhanced!

It is a beautiful image which tells us that the Church is like a great orchestra in which there is great variety. We are not all the same and we do not all have to be the same. We are all different, varied, each of us with his own special qualities. And this is the beauty of the Church: everyone brings his own gift, which God has given him, for the sake of enriching others. And between the various components there is diversity; however, it is a diversity that does not enter into conflict and opposition. It is a variety that allows the Holy Spirit to blend it into harmony. He is the true "Maestro." He is harmony. And here let us ask ourselves: in our communities do we live in harmony or do we argue amongst ourselves? In my parish community, in my movement, in the place where I am part of the Church, is there gossip? If there is gossip, there is no harmony but rather conflict. And this is not the Church. The Church is everyone in harmony: never gossip about others, never argue! Let us accept others, let us accept that there is a fitting variety, that this person is different, that this person thinks about things in this way or that—that within one and the same faith we can think about things differently—or do we tend to make everything uniform? But uniformity kills life. The life of the Church is variety,

> **This is the beauty of the Church: everyone brings his own gift, which God has given him, for the sake of enriching others.**

9

and when we want to impose this uniformity on everyone we kill the gifts of the Holy Spirit.

Let us pray to the Holy Spirit, who is truly the author of this unity in variety, of this harmony, that he might make us ever more "catholic" in this Church which is catholic and universal! Thank you.

✤

I cordially greet all the English-speaking pilgrims present at today's Audience . . . Upon all of you, and your families, I invoke God's blessings of joy and peace!

Dear Arabic-speaking faithful, one year ago, October 10, 2012, Pope Benedict, after his Journey to Lebanon and consigning of the Apostolic Exhortation, *The Church in the Middle East: Communion and Witness*, he introduced the Arabic language to the General Audience, as requested by the Synod Fathers, in order to express to all Christians of the Middle East the closeness of the Catholic Church to her children in the East. And today by speaking of the expression: "I believe in the Catholic Church," I ask you to pray for peace in the Middle East: in Syria, in Iraq, in Egypt, in Lebanon and in the Holy Land where the Prince of Peace, Jesus Christ, was born. Pray that the light of Christ reach every heart and every place to the ends of the earth. The blessing of the Lord be with you always!

Then I turn my thoughts to the *young people*, to *the sick* and to *newlyweds*. I thank all of you for coming to this meeting, and I encourage you to listen to the "wounds of Jesus," through a caring attention to the weakest and most in need. . . .

MARIAN DAY

OCTOBER 13, 2013

ST. PETER'S SQUARE

Dear Brothers and Sisters,

Today in Tarragona, Spain approximately 500 martyrs who were killed for the faith during the Spanish Civil War in the 1930s are being beatified. We praise the Lord for their courageous witness; through their intercession let us ask him to free the world from every form of violence.

I wish to thank all of you who have come out in such great numbers . . . from so many parts of the world for this celebration of faith dedicated to Mary, our Mother. . . .

I also greet the youth . . . always be missionaries of the Gospel, every day and in every place! . . .

I wish you a blessed Sunday, have a nice lunch. Goodbye!

THE CHURCH IS APOSTOLIC

OCTOBER 16, 2013

ST. PETER'S SQUARE

Dear Brothers and Sisters, good morning!

When we recite the Creed we say "I believe in one, holy, catholic and apostolic Church." I don't know if you have ever reflected on the meaning of the expression "the Church is apostolic." Perhaps from time to time, coming to Rome, you have thought about the importance of the Apostles Peter and Paul who here gave their lives to bring and bear witness to the Gospel.

But it is even more. To profess that the Church is apostolic means to stress the constitutive bond that she has with the Apostles, with that small group of twelve men whom Jesus one day called to himself, he called them by name, that they might remain with him and that he might

13

send them out to preach (cf. Mk 3:13-19). "Apostle," in fact, is a Greek word meaning "sent," "dispatched." An Apostle is a person who has been given a mandate, he is sent to do something and the Apostles were chosen, called and sent out by Jesus to continue his work, that is to pray—which is the primary job of an apostle—and, second, to proclaim the Gospel. This is important, because when we think of the Apostles we might think that they were only sent out to proclaim the Gospel, to do many good deeds. However, a problem arose in the early times of the Church because of how much the Apostles had to do, and that is why they instituted deacons, so that there would be more time for the Apostles to pray and proclaim the Word of God. When we think of the Successors of the Apostles, the bishops—this includes the Pope for he too is a bishop—we must ask ourselves if this successor of the Apostles prays first and then proclaims the Gospel: this is what it means to be an Apostle and this is what makes the Church apostolic. Every one of us, if we want to be apostles as I shall explain now, must ask ourselves: do I pray for the salvation of the world? Do I proclaim the Gospel? This is the Church apostolic! It is the constitutive bond that we have with the Apostles.

Starting from this I would like to focus briefly on the three meanings of the adjective "apostolic" as it is applied to the Church.

1. The Church is apostolic because she is *founded on the preaching and prayer of the Apostles*, on the authority

that was entrusted to them by Christ himself. St. Paul writes to the Christians of Ephesus: "You are no longer strangers and sojourners, but you are fellow citizens with the saints and members of the household of God, built upon the foundation of the apostles and prophets, Christ Jesus himself being a cornerstone" (Eph 2:19-20); that is, he compares Christians to living stones that form an edifice that is the Church, and this edifice is founded on the Apostles, like columns, and the cornerstone that carries it all is Jesus himself. Without Jesus the Church cannot exist! Jesus is the foundation

Every one of us, if we want to be apostles, must ask ourselves: do I pray for the salvation of the world?

of the Church, the foundation! The Apostles lived with Jesus, they listened to his words, they shared his life, above all they were witnesses of his Death and Resurrection. Our faith, the Church that Christ willed, is not based on an idea, it is not based on a philosophy, it is based on Christ himself. And the Church is like a plant that over the long centuries has grown, has developed, has borne fruit, yet her roots are planted firmly in Him and that fundamental experience of Christ which the Apostles had, chosen and sent out by Jesus, reaching all the way to us.

From this little plant to our day: this is how the Church has spread everywhere in the world.

2. But let us ask ourselves: how is it possible for us to be connected to that testimony, how could what the Apostles' experienced with Jesus, what they heard from him reach us? This is the second meaning of the term "apostolic." *The Catechism of the Catholic Church* states that the Church is apostolic because "with the help of the Spirit dwelling in her, the Church *keeps and hands on* the teaching, the 'good deposit,' the salutary words she has heard from the Apostles" (no. 857). Over the centuries, the Church conserves this precious treasure, which is Sacred Scripture, doctrine, the Sacraments, the ministry of Pastors, so that we can be faithful to Christ and share in his very life. It is like a river coursing through history, developing, irrigating; but running water always comes from a source, and the source is Christ himself: he is the Risen One, he is the Living One, and his words never pass away, for he does not pass, he is alive, he is among us today, he hears us and we speak to him and he listens, he is in our hearts. Jesus is with us today! This is the beauty of the Church: the presence of Jesus Christ among us. Do we ever think about how important this gift that Jesus gave us is, the gift of the Church, where we can meet him? Do we ever think about how it is precisely the Church on her journey through the centuries—despite the difficulties, the problems, the weaknesses, our sins— that transmits to us the authentic message of Christ? She

gives us the certainty that what we believe in is really what Christ communicated to us?

3. My final thought: the Church is apostolic because she is *sent to bring the Gospel to all the world.* She continues in history the mission which Jesus entrusted to the Apostles: "Go therefore and make disciples of all nations, baptizing them in the name of the Father and of the Son and of the Holy Spirit, teaching them to observe all that I have commanded you; and lo, I am with you always, to the close of the age" (Mt 28:19-20). This is what Jesus told us to do! I insist on this missionary aspect, because Christ invites all to "go out" and encounter others, he sends us, he asks us to move in order to spread the joy of the Gospel! Once again let

Christ invites all to "go out" and encounter others, he sends us, he asks us to move in order to spread the joy of the Gospel!

us ask ourselves: are we missionaries by our words, and especially by our Christian life, by our witness? Or are we Christians closed in our hearts and in our churches, sacristy Christians? Are we Christians in name only, who live like pagans? We must ask ourselves these questions, which are not a rebuke. I ask myself as well: what kind of Christian am I, is my witness true?

The Church's roots are in the teaching of the Apostles, the authentic witnesses of Christ, but she looks to the future, she has the firm consciousness of being sent—sent by Jesus—of being missionary, bearing the name of Jesus by her prayer, proclaiming it and testifying to it. A Church that is closed in on herself and in the past, a Church that only sees the little rules of behavior, of attitude, is a Church that betrays her own identity; a closed Church betrays her own identity! Then, let us rediscover today all the beauty and responsibility of being the Church apostolic! And remember this: the Church is apostolic because we pray—our first duty—and because we proclaim the Gospel by our life and by our words.

I cordially greet all the English-speaking pilgrims present at today's Audience . . . Upon all of you, and your families, I invoke God's blessings of joy and peace!

Finally, an affectionate thought to *young people*, to the *sick* and to *newlyweds*. Today we celebrate the memory of St. Margaret Mary Alacoque. May her devotion to the Sacred Heart of Jesus instruct you, dear *young people* . . . to love as he loved; may it make you strong, dear *sick* people, in carrying your cross of suffering with patience; and may it sustain you, dear *newlyweds*, in building your family upon fidelity and dedication.

PERSEVERE IN PRAYER

OCTOBER 20, 2013

ST. PETER'S SQUARE

Dear Brothers and Sisters,

In today's Gospel Jesus tells a parable on the need to pray always, never wearying. The main character is a widow whose insistent pleading with a dishonest judge succeeds in obtaining justice from him. Jesus concludes: if the widow succeeded in convincing that judge, do you think that God will not listen to us if we pray to him with insistence? Jesus' words are very strong: "And will not God vindicate his elect, who cry to him day and night?" (Lk 18:7).

"Crying day and night" to God! This image of prayer is striking, but let us ask ourselves: Why does God want this? Doesn't he already know what we need? What does it mean to "insist" with God?

This is a good question that makes us examine an important aspect of the faith: God invites us to pray insistently not because he is unaware of our needs or because he is not listening to us. On the contrary, he is always listening and he knows everything about us lovingly. On our daily journey, especially in times of difficulty, in the battle against the evil that is outside and within us, the Lord is not far away, he is by our side. We battle with him beside us, and our weapon is prayer which makes us feel his presence beside us, his mercy and also his help. But the battle against evil is a long and hard one; it requires patience and endurance, like Moses who had to keep his arms outstretched for the people to prevail (cf. Ex 17:8-13). This is how it is: there is a battle to be waged each day, but God is our ally, faith in him is our strength and prayer is the expression of this faith. Therefore Jesus assures us of the victory, but at the end he asks: "when the Son of man comes, will he find faith on earth?" (Lk 18:8). If faith is snuffed out, prayer is snuffed out, and we walk in the dark. We become lost on the path of life.

....

There is a battle to be waged each day, but God is our ally, faith in him is our strength and prayer is the expression of this faith.

Therefore, let us learn from the widow of the Gospel to pray always without growing weary. This widow was very good! She knew how to battle for her children! I think of the many women who fight for their families, who pray and never grow weary. Today let us all remember these women who by their attitude provide us with a true witness of faith and courage, and a model of prayer. Our thoughts go out to them!

Pray always, but not in order to convince the Lord by dint of words! He knows our needs better than we do! Indeed persevering prayer is the expression of faith in a God who calls us to fight with him every day and at every moment in order to conquer evil with good.

Dear brothers and sisters, today is World Mission Sunday. What is the mission of the Church? To spread throughout the world the flame of faith which Jesus kindled in the world: faith in God who is Father, Love, Mercy. The method of Christian mission is not proselytism but rather that of sharing the flame that warms the soul. I wish to thank all those who through their prayer and practical help support missionary work, especially the work of the Bishop of Rome to spread the Gospel. On this Day, we are close to all men and women missionaries who work so hard without making any noise and who give their lives, like the Italian missionary Afra Martinelli who worked for many years in Nigeria. Some days ago she was killed during a robbery. Everyone mourned her loss, Christians and Muslims. They loved her. She proclaimed the Gospel with her life, with the work she carried out at the educational center she had set up. In this way she spread the flame of faith, and fought the good fight! Let us think of our sister of ours and let us all remember her with a round of applause!

My thoughts also turn to Stefano Sándor, who was beatified in Budapest yesterday. He was a Salesian layman and a model of service to youth in the oratory and in his profession as a teacher. When the communist regime closed all Catholic institutions, he courageously faced persecution and was killed at the age of thirty-nine. We join in giving thanks to the Salesian family and the Church in Hungary.

I wish to express my closeness to the peoples of the Philippines who have been struck by a severe earthquake, and I invite you to pray for that dear nation which recently has undergone various calamities.

I warmly greet all of the pilgrims present here, beginning with the young people who participated in the "100 meter sprint for faith" sponsored by the Pontifical Council for Culture. Thank you, for you remind us that the believer is a spiritual athlete! Thank you very much!

Have a blessed Sunday! Goodbye and have a good lunch!

MARY, MODEL OF THE CHURCH

OCTOBER 23, 2013

ST. PETER'S SQUARE

Dear Brothers and Sisters, good morning!

Continuing our catecheses on the Church, today I would like to look at Mary as the image and model of the Church. I will do so by taking up an expression of the Second Vatican Council. The Constitution *Lumen Gentium* states: "As St. Ambrose taught, the Mother of God is a type of the Church in the order of faith, charity, and the perfect union with Christ" (no. 63).

1. Let us begin with the first aspect, *Mary as the model of faith.* In what sense does Mary represent a model for the Church's faith? Let us think about who the Virgin Mary was: a Jewish girl who was waiting with all her heart for the redemption of her people. But in the heart of the

young daughter of Israel there was a secret that even she herself did not yet know: in God's loving plan she was destined to become the Mother of the Redeemer. At the Annunciation, the Messenger of God calls her "full of grace" and reveals this plan to her. Mary answers "yes" and from that moment Mary's faith receives new light: it is concentrated on Jesus, the Son of God, who from her took flesh and in whom all the promises of salvation history are fulfilled. Mary's faith is the fulfilment of Israel's faith, the whole journey, the whole path of that people awaiting redemption is contained in her, and it is in this sense that she is the model of the Church's faith, which has Christ, the incarnation of God's infinite love, as its center.

How did Mary live this faith? She lived it out in the simplicity of the thousand daily tasks and worries of every mother, such as providing food, clothing, caring for the house. . . . It was precisely Our Lady's normal life which served as the basis for the unique relationship and profound dialogue which unfolded between her and God, between her and her Son. Mary's "yes," already perfect from the start, grew until the hour of the Cross. There her motherhood opened to embrace every one of us, our lives, so as to guide us to her Son. Mary lived perpetually immersed in the mystery of God-made-man, as his first and perfect disciple, by contemplating all things in her heart in the light of the Holy Spirit, in order to understand and live out the will of God.

We can ask ourselves a question: do we allow ourselves to be illumined by the faith of Mary, who is our Mother? Or do we think of her as distant, as someone too different from us? In moments of difficulty, of trial, of darkness, do we look to her as a model of trust in God who always and only desires our good? Let's think about this: perhaps it will do us good to rediscover Mary as the model and figure of the Church in this faith that she possessed!

2. We come to the second aspect: *Mary as the model of charity*. In what way is Mary a living example of love for the Church? Let us think the readiness she showed toward her cousin Elizabeth. In visiting her, the Virgin Mary brought not only material help— she brought this too—but she also brought Jesus, who was already alive in her womb. Bringing Jesus into that house meant bringing joy, the fullness

In moments of difficulty, of trial, of darkness, do we look to Mary as a model of trust in God who always and only desires our good?

of joy. Elizabeth and Zaccariah were rejoicing at a pregnancy that had seemed impossible at their age, but it was the young Mary who brought them the fullness of joy, the joy which comes from Jesus and from the Holy Spirit, and is expressed by gratuitous charity, by sharing with, helping, and understanding others.

Our Lady also wants to bring the great gift of Jesus to us, to us all; and with him she brings us his love, his peace, and his joy. In this, the Church is like Mary: the Church is not a shop, she is not a humanitarian agency, the Church is not an NGO. The Church is sent to bring Christ and his Gospel to all. She does not bring herself—whether small or great, strong or weak, the Church carries Jesus and should be like Mary when she went to visit Elizabeth. What did Mary take to her? Jesus. The Church brings Jesus: this is the center of the Church, to carry Jesus! If, as a hypothesis, the Church were not to bring Jesus, she would be a dead Church. The Church must bring Jesus, the love of Jesus, the charity of Jesus.

We have spoken about Mary, about Jesus. What about us? We who are the Church? What kind of love do we bring to others? Is it the love of Jesus that shares, that forgives, that accompanies, or is it a watered-down love, like wine so diluted that it seems like water? Is it a strong love, or a love so weak that it follows the emotions, that it seeks a return, an interested love? Another question: is self-interested love pleasing to Jesus? No, it is not because love should be freely given, like his is. What are the relationships like in our parishes, in our communities? Do we treat each other like brothers and sisters? Or do we judge one another, do we speak evil of one another, do we just tend our own vegetable patch? Or do we care for one another? These are the questions of charity!

3. And briefly, one last aspect: *Mary as the model of union with Christ*. The life of the Holy Virgin was the life of a woman of her people: Mary prayed, she worked, she went to the synagogue . . . But every action was carried out in perfect union with Jesus. This union finds its culmination on Calvary: here Mary is united to the Son in the martyrdom of her heart and in the offering of his life to the Father for the salvation of humanity. Our Lady shared in the pain of the Son and accepted with him the will of the Father, in that obedience that bears fruit, that grants the true victory over evil and death.

....

What kind of love do we bring to others? Is it the love of Jesus that shares, that forgives, that accompanies, or is it a watered-down love, like wine so diluted that it seems like water?

The reality Mary teaches us is very beautiful: to always be united with Jesus. We can ask ourselves: do we remember Jesus only when something goes wrong and we are in need, or is ours a constant relation, a deep friendship, even when it means following him on the way of the Cross?

Let us ask the Lord to grant us his grace, his strength, so that the model of Mary, Mother of the Church, may be reflected in our lives and in the life of every ecclesial community. So be it!

꧁꧂

I greet all the English-speaking pilgrims present at today's Audience . . . Upon all of you, and your families, I invoke God's blessings of joy and peace!

Lastly, an affectionate thought goes to *young people*, the *sick* and *newlyweds*. The month of October reminds us of each person's part in the mission to proclaim the Gospel. Dear *young people*, . . . may you be courageous witnesses of the Christian faith: dear *sick people*, offer your daily cross for the conversion of those far from the Gospel; and you, dear *newlyweds*, announce the love of Christ beginning with your families.

MARY, QUEEN OF THE FAMILY

OCTOBER 27, 2013

ST. PETER'S SQUARE

Before concluding this celebration, I wish to greet all pilgrims, especially all of you, dear families, who have come from many countries. Thank you very much! . . .

I extend a cordial greeting to the Bishops and to the faithful from the Republic of Equatorial Guinea, who are gathered here on the occasion of the ratification of the Agreement with the Holy See. The Immaculate Virgin protects your beloved people and helps you to move forward on the path of harmony and justice.

Now let us pray . . . we invoke the maternal protection of Mary for families all around the world, and in a particular way for those who live in situations of great difficulty. Mary, Queen of the Family, pray for us! Let us say together: Mary, Queen of the Family, Pray for us!

Mary Queen of the Family, Pray for us! Mary, Queen of the Family, pray for us! . . .

Thank you very much for yesterday's celebration and for this Mass. May God bless you all. I wish you a good Sunday and a good lunch. Goodbye!

THE COMMUNION
OF SAINTS

OCTOBER 30, 2013

ST. PETER'S SQUARE

Dear Brothers and Sisters, good morning!

Today I would like to speak about a very beautiful reality of our faith, namely, the "communion of saints." The *Catechism of the Catholic Church* reminds us that two realities are meant by this expression: communion 'in holy things' and 'among holy persons' (no. 948). I wish to pause on the second meaning: this is one of the most consoling truths of our faith, since it reminds us that we are not alone but that there is a communion of life among all those who belong to Christ. It is a communion that is born of faith; indeed, the term "saints" refers to those who believe in the Lord Jesus and are incorporated by him into the Church through Baptism. That is why the first Christians were also called "saints" (cf. Acts 9:13, 32, 41; Rm 8:27; 1 Cor 6:1).

1. John's Gospel states that, before his Passion, Jesus prayed to the Father for communion among his disciples, with these words: "that they may all be one; even as thou, Father, art in me, and I in thee, that they also may be in us, so that the world may believe that thou hast sent me" (17:21). The Church, in her most profound truth, is *communion with God*, intimacy with God, a communion of love with Christ and with the Father in the Holy Spirit, which extends to brotherly communion. This relationship between Jesus and the Father is the "matrix" of the bond between us Christians: if we are intimately part of this "matrix," this fiery furnace of love, then we can truly become of one single heart and one single soul among us. For God's love burns away our selfishness, our prejudices, our interior and exterior divisions. The love of God even burns away our sins.

2. If we are rooted in the source of Love, which is God, then a reciprocal movement also occurs: from brothers to God. The experience of fraternal communion leads me to communion with God. Union among us leads to union with God, it leads us to this bond with God who is our Father. This is the second aspect of the communion of saints that I would like to underline: *our faith needs the support of others*, especially in difficult moments. If we are united our faith becomes stronger. How beautiful it is to support each other in the wonderful adventure of faith! I

say this because the tendency to be closed and private has influenced the religious sphere as well, so much so that it often becomes difficult to ask for spiritual help from those would share this Christian life with us. Who among us has not experienced insecurity, confusion and even doubt on our journey of faith? We have all experienced this, myself as well. It is part of the journey of faith, it is part of our life. None of this should surprise us, because we are humans beings, marked by fragility and limitations. We are all frail, we all have limitations. Nevertheless, in these difficult moments it is necessary to trust in God's help, through child-like prayer, and, at the same time, it is important to find the courage and the humility to open up to others, to ask for help, to ask for a helping hand. How often have we done this and then succeeded in emerging from our difficulty and finding God again! In this communion—communion means common-union— we form a great family, where every member is helped and sustained by the others.

3. And we come to another aspect: the communion of saints goes *beyond earthly life, beyond death and endures for ever*. This union among us goes beyond and continues in the next life; it is a spiritual communion born in Baptism and not broken by death, but, thanks to the Risen Christ, is destined to find its fullness in eternal life. There is a deep and indissoluble bond between those who are still pilgrims in this world—us—and those who have crossed the threshold of death and entered eternity. All baptized

persons here on earth, the souls in Purgatory and all the blessed who are already in Paradise make one great Family. This communion between earth and heaven is realized especially in intercessory prayer.

Dear friends, we have this beauty! This is our reality, all of ours, that makes us brothers and sisters, that accompanies us on the journey of life and lets us find another face above in heaven. Let us go forward on this journey with trust, with joy. A Christian must be joyful, with the joy of having so many baptized brothers and sisters to journey with him; sustained by the help of brothers and sisters who are taking the same path toward heaven; and also by the help of brothers and sisters who are in heaven and are praying to Jesus for us. Go forward on this path with joy!

I greet all the English-speaking pilgrims present at today's Audience . . . I invoke God's blessings of joy and peace!

Lastly, I greet the sick, newlyweds and young people . . . This Friday we will celebrate the Solemnity of All Saints. May their witness of faith strengthen in each of you, dear young people, the certainty that God is with you on the journey of life; may it sustain you, dear sick people, by alleviating your daily suffering; and may it be of help to you, dear newlyweds, in building your family on faith in God.

HOLINESS IS A CALLING FOR EVERYONE

Solemnity of All Saints

November 1, 2013

St. Peter's Square

Dear Brothers and Sisters, good morning!

The Feast of All Saints that we are celebrating today reminds us that the goal of our existence is not death, it is Paradise! The Apostle John writes: "it does not yet appear what we shall be, but we know that when he appears we shall be like him, for we shall see him as he is" (1 Jn 3:2). The Saints—who are the friends of God—assure us of this promise which does not disappoint. During their earthly existence they lived in profound communion with God.

In the faces of the humblest and least of our brothers, the smallest and most despised brothers, they saw the face of God, and now they contemplate him face to face in his glorious beauty.

The Saints are not supermen, nor were they born perfect. They are like us, like each one of us. They are people who, before reaching the glory of heaven, lived normal lives with joys and sorrows, struggles and hopes. What changed their lives? When they recognized God's love, they followed it with all their heart without reserve or hypocrisy. They spent their lives serving others, they endured suffering and adversity without hatred and responded to evil with good, spreading joy and peace. This is the life of a Saint. Saints are people who for love of God did not put conditions on him in their life; they were not hypocrites; they spent their lives at the service of others. They suffered much adversity but without hate. The Saints never hated. Understand this well: love is of God, then from whom does hatred come? Hatred does not come from God but from the devil! And the Saints removed themselves from the devil; the Saints are men and women who have joy in their hearts and they spread

> **The Saints are not supermen, nor were they born perfect. They are like us, like each one of us.**

it to others. Never hate but serve others, the most needy; pray and live in joy. This is the way of holiness!

Being holy is not a privilege for the few, as if someone had a large inheritance; in Baptism we all have an inheritance to be able to become saints. Holiness is a vocation for everyone. Thus we are all called to walk on the path of holiness, and this path has a name and a face: the face of Jesus Christ. He teaches us to become saints. In the Gospel he shows us the way, the way of the Beatitudes (cf. Mt 5:1-12). In fact, the Kingdom of Heaven is for those who do not place their security in material things but in love for God, for those who have a simple, humble heart that does not presume to be just and does not judge others, for those who know how to suffer with those who suffer and how to rejoice when others rejoice. They are not violent but merciful and strive to be instruments for reconciliation and peace. Saints, whether men or women, are instruments for reconciliation and peace; they are always helping people to become reconciled and helping to bring about peace. Thus holiness is beautiful, it is a beautiful path!

Today, through this feast, the Saints give us a message. They tell us: trust in the Lord because the Lord does not disappoint! He never disappoints, he is a good friend always at our side. Through their witness the Saints encourage us to not be afraid of going against the tide or of being misunderstood and mocked when we speak about him and the Gospel; by their life they show us that he who stays faithful to God and to his Word experiences the comfort of his love on this earth and then a "hundredfold" in eternity. This is what we hope for and ask of the Lord, for our deceased brothers and sisters. With her wisdom the Church has placed the Feast of All Saints and All Souls' Day near each other. May our prayer of praise to God and veneration of the blessed spirits join with the prayer of suffrage for the souls of those who have preceded us in the passage from this world to eternal life.

Let us entrust our prayers to the intercession of Mary, Queen of All Saints.

Dear brothers and sisters,

I warmly greet everyone especially the families, parish groups and associations.

I express a very warm greeting to those who participated this morning in the "Race of Saints" organized by the Don Bosco in the World Foundation. St. Paul would say that the whole life of a Christian is a "race" to gain the prize of holiness: you give us a good example! Thank you for this race!

This afternoon I shall go to Verano Cemetery and celebrate Holy Mass there. I will spiritually join those who in these days are visiting cemeteries, the place of rest for those who preceded us in the sign of faith and who wait for the day of resurrection. In particular I will pray for victims of violence especially for the Christians who have lost their lives due to persecution. I will also pray in a special way for our brothers and sisters, men, women and children who have died of thirst, hunger or from the exhaustion on the journey to find a better life. In recent days we have seen those terrible images of the desert in the newspapers. Let us all pray in silence for these brothers and sisters of ours.

I wish everyone a happy Feast of All Saints. Goodbye and have a good lunch!

I MUST STAY AT YOUR HOUSE TODAY!

NOVEMBER 3, 2013

ST. PETER'S SQUARE

Dear Brothers and Sisters, good morning!

The page of Luke's Gospel chosen for this Sunday shows us Jesus who, on his way to Jerusalem, enters the city of Jericho. This is the final stage of a journey that sums up the meaning of the whole of Jesus' life, which was dedicated to searching and saving the lost sheep of the house of Israel. But the more the journey comes to a close, the more hostility envelops Jesus.

Yet one of the most joyful events recounted by St. Luke happens in Jericho: the conversion of Zacchaeus. This man is a lost sheep, he is despised and "excommunicated" because he is a tax collector, indeed he is the head of the tax collectors of the city, a friend of the hated Roman occupants; he is a thief and an exploiter.

Being short in stature and prevented from approaching Jesus, most likely because of his bad reputation, Zacchaeus climbs a tree to be able to see the Teacher who is passing by. This exterior action, which is a bit ridiculous, expresses the interior act of a man seeking to bring himself above the crowd in order to be near Jesus. Zacchaeus himself does not realize the deep meaning of his action; he doesn't understand why he does it, but he does. Nor does he dare to hope that the distance which separates him from the Lord may be overcome; he resigns himself to seeing him only as he passes by. But when Jesus comes close to the tree he calls him by name: "Zacchaeus, make haste and come down; for I must stay at your house today" (Lk 19:5). The man of small stature, rejected by everyone and far from Jesus, is lost in anonymity; but Jesus calls him. And the name "Zacchaeus" in the language of the time has a beautiful meaning, full of allusion. "Zacchaeus" in fact, means "God remembers."

So Jesus goes to Zacchaeus' house, drawing criticism from all the people of Jericho (even in those days there was a lot of gossip!), who said: How can this be? With all the good people in the city, how can he go stay with a tax collector? Yes, because he was lost. Jesus said: "Today salvation has come to this house, since he is also a son of Abraham" (Lk 19:9). From that day forward in Zacchaeus' house joy entered, peace entered, salvation entered and Jesus entered.

There is no profession or social condition, no sin or crime of any kind that can erase from the memory and the heart of God even one of his children. "God remembers," always, he never forgets those who he created. He is the Father, who watchfully and lovingly waits to see the

....

There is no profession or social condition, no sin or crime of any kind that can erase from the memory and the heart of God even one of his children.

desire to return home be reborn in the hearts of his children. And when he sees this desire, even simply hinted at and so often almost unconsciously, immediately he is there, and by his forgiveness he lightens the path of conversion and return. Let us look at Zacchaeus today in the tree: his is a ridiculous act but it is an act of

salvation. And I say to you: if your conscience is weighed down, if you are ashamed of many things that you have done, stop for a moment, do not be afraid. Think about the fact that someone is waiting for you because he has never ceased to remember you; and this someone is your Father, it is God who is waiting for you! Climb up, as Zacchaeus did, climb the tree of desire for forgiveness. I assure you that you will not be disappointed. Jesus is merciful and never grows tired of forgiving! Remember that this is the way Jesus is.

Brothers and sisters, let Jesus also call us by name! In the depths of our hearts, let us listen to his voice which says: "Today I must stop at your house"; that is, in your heart, in your life. And let us welcome him with joy. He can change us, he can transform our stoney hearts into hearts of flesh, he can free us from selfishness and make our lives a gift of love. Jesus can do this; let Jesus turn his gaze to you!

Dear brothers and sisters,

I greet with affection . . . pilgrims who are present, in particular families, parishes, and the groups from many countries all over the world.

I wish everyone a good Sunday and a good lunch. Goodbye!

COMMUNION IN HOLY THINGS

NOVEMBER 6, 2013

ST. PETER'S SQUARE

Dear Brothers and Sisters, good morning!

Last Wednesday I spoke about the communion of saints, understood as a communion among holy people, that is among us believers. Today I would like to go in depth into the other aspect of this reality: you will remember that there were two aspects: one is communion, unity, among us, and the other aspect is communion in holy things, *in spiritual goods*. These two aspects are closely connected; in fact, communion among Christians grows through the sharing of spiritual goods. In particular we will consider: *the Sacraments, charisms and charity* (cf. *The Catechism of the Catholic Church*, nos. 949-953). We grow in unity, in communion, through: the Sacraments, the charisms given to each of us by the Holy Spirit, and charity.

First of all, the *communion of the Sacraments*. The Sacraments express and realize an effective and profound communion among us, for in them we encounter Christ the Savior and, through him, our brothers and sisters in faith. The Sacraments are not mere appearances, they are not rituals; they are the power of Christ; Jesus Christ is present in the Sacraments. When we celebrate the Eucharist it is the living Jesus who brings us together, forms us into a community, allows us to adore the Father. Each one of us, in fact, through Baptism, Confirmation and the Eucharist, is incorporated into Christ and united to the entire community of

....

The Sacraments are not mere appearances, they are not rituals; they are the power of Christ; Jesus Christ is present in the Sacraments.

believers. Therefore, if on the one hand it is the Church that "makes" the Sacraments, on the other, it is the Sacraments that "make" the Church, that build her up, by generating new children, by gathering them into the holy people of God, by strengthening their membership.

Every encounter with Christ, who in the Sacraments gives us salvation, invites us to "go" and communicate to others the salvation that we have been able to see, to touch, to encounter and to receive, and which is truly credible because it is love. In this way, the Sacraments spur us to be missionaries, and the Apostolic commitment to carry the Gospel into every setting, including those most hostile, is the most authentic fruit of an assiduous sacramental life, since it is a participation in the saving initiative of God, who desires salvation for all people. The grace of the Sacraments nourishes in us a strong and joyful faith, a faith that knows how to stand in wonder before the "marvels" of God and how to resist the idols of the world. That is why it is important to take Communion, it is important that children be baptized early, that they be confirmed, because the Sacraments are the presence of Jesus Christ in us, a presence that helps us. It is important, when we feel the weight of our sin to approach the Sacrament of Reconciliation. Someone might say: "But I am afraid that the priest will chastise me." No, the priest will not chastise you. Do you know who you will encounter in the Sacrament of Reconciliation? You will encounter Jesus who pardons you! Jesus is waiting for you there; and this is a Sacrament that makes the whole Church grow.

A second aspect of communion in holy things is the *communion of charisms*. The Holy Spirit distributes to the faithful a multitude of spiritual gifts and graces; the "imaginative" wealth, let us say, of gifts of the Holy Spirit is ordered to building up the Church. The charisms—that word is a little difficult—are gifts that the Holy

Spirit gives us, talents, possibilities. . . . Gifts given not to be hidden but to be shared with others. They are not given for the benefit of the one who receives them, but for the use of the People of God. If a charism, one of these gifts, serves instead as self-affirmation, then it is doubtful that we are dealing with an authentic charism or one faithfully lived out. The charisms are special graces, given to some for the good of many others. They are attitudes, inspirations and interior promptings that are born in the consciences and experiences of certain people, who are called to put themselves at the service of the community. In particular, these spiritual gifts further the sanctity of the Church and her mission. We are all called to respect them in ourselves and in others, to receive them as serving the Church's fruitful presence and work. St. Paul warns: "Do not quench the Holy Spirit" (1 Thes 5:19). Let us not quench the Spirit who gives us these gifts, these abilities, these very beautiful virtues that make the Church grow.

Do you know who you will encounter in the Sacrament of Reconciliation? You will encounter Jesus who pardons you! Jesus is waiting for you there; and this is a Sacrament that makes the whole Church grow.

What is our attitude to the gifts of the Holy Spirit? Are we aware that the Spirit of God is free to give them to whomsoever he wishes? Do we consider them as a spiritual help, through which the Lord sustains our faith and reinforces our mission in the world?

And we come to the third aspect of communion in holy things, that is, *communion in charity*, the unity among us that creates charity, love. The gentiles, observing the early Christians, said: how they love each other, how they wish one another well! They do not hate, they do not speak against one another. This is the charity, the love of God that the Holy Spirit puts in our hearts. The charisms are important in the life of the Christian community, but they are always a means for growth in charity, in love, which St. Paul sets above the charisms (cf. 1 Cor 13:1-13). Without love, in fact, even the most extraordinary gifts are in vain; this man heals people, he has that power, this other virtue . . . but does he have love and charity in his heart? If he does then all is well, but if he does not he is no servant of the Church. Without love no gift or charism could serve the Church, for where there is not love there is an emptiness that becomes filled with selfishness. And I ask myself: if we all were egotistical, could we live in communion and peace? No, it's not possible, that is why it is necessary that love unite us. Our smallest gesture of love benefits everyone! Therefore, to live out unity in the Church and communion in charity means not seeking one's own interests but sharing the suffering and the joy of one's brothers (cf. 1 Cor 12:26), ready to carry the weight of the poorest and the weakest. This fraternal solidarity is not a figure of speech, a saying, but an integral part of the communion among Christians. If we live it, we are a sign to the world, the "sacrament" of God's love. This is what we are one for another and what we are for all! It is not just petty love that we can offer one another, but something

....

Without love no gift or charism could serve the Church, for where there is not love there is an emptiness that becomes filled with selfishness.

much more profound: it is a communion that renders us capable of entering into the joy and sorrow of others and making them sincerely our own.

Often we are too dry, indifferent and detached and rather than transmitting brotherhood, we communicate bad temper, coldness and selfishness. And with bad temper, coldness and selfishness the Church cannot grow; the Church grows only by the love that comes from the Holy Spirit. The Lord invites us to open ourselves to communion with him, in the Sacraments, in the charisms and in charity, in order to live out our Christian vocation with dignity!

And now let me ask you for an act of charity: relax, it is not a collection! Before coming into the Square I went to see a little girl, a year and half old, who is gravely ill. Her father and mother are praying, and asking the Lord to heal this beautiful little girl. Her name is Noemi. The poor little one was smiling! Let us perform an act of love. We do not know her, but she is a baptized child, she is one of us, she is a Christian. Let us perform an act of love for her and in silence ask the Lord for his help in this moment and that he grant her health. Let us take a moment of silence and then we will pray the "Hail Mary." And now all together let us pray to Our Lady for the health of Noemi. *Hail Mary* . . . Thank you for this act of charity.

I greet all the English-speaking pilgrims present at today's Audience . . . I also thank the choirs present for their praise of God in song. Upon all of you, and your families, I invoke God's blessings of joy and peace!

Lastly, I greet *young people*, the *sick* and *newlyweds*. The month of November, dedicated to the memory of and prayer for the deceased, offers us the opportunity to consider more deeply the meaning of earthly life and the value of eternal life. May these days be for you all a stimulus to understanding that life has value if it is spent loving God and neighbor.

ON THE JOURNEY TO EVERLASTING LIFE

NOVEMBER 10, 2013

ST. PETER'S SQUARE

Dear Brothers and Sisters, good morning!

This Sunday's Gospel sets before us Jesus grappling with the Sadducees, who deny that there is a resurrection. They pose a question to Jesus on this very matter, in order to trip him up and ridicule faith in the resurrection of the dead. They begin with an imaginary case: "A woman had seven husbands, who died one after the other," and they ask Jesus: "Whose wife will the woman be after her death?" Jesus, ever meek and patient, first replies that life after death does not have the same parameters as earthly life. Eternal life is another life, in another dimension where, among other things, there will be no marriage, which is tied to our existence in this world. Those who rise—Jesus says—will be like the angels and they will live in a different state, which now we can neither experience nor imagine. This is the way Jesus explains it.

But then Jesus, as it were, moves to the counterattack. And he does so by citing the Sacred Scripture with a simplicity and originality which leaves us full of admiration for our Teacher, the only Teacher! Jesus finds proof for the resurrection in the account of Moses and the burning bush (cf. Ex 3:1-6), where God reveals himself as the God of Abraham, and of Isaac and of Jacob. The name of God is bound to the names of men and women to whom he binds himself, and this bond is stronger than death. And we can also say this about God's relationship with us, with each one of us: He is *our* God! He is the God of each one of us! As though he bore each of our names. It pleases him to say it, and this is the covenant. This is why Jesus states: "God is not the god of the dead, but of the living; for all live to him" (Lk 20:38). And this is the decisive bond, the fundamental covenant, the covenant with Jesus: He himself is the Covenant, he himself is the Life and the Resurrection, for by his crucified love he has triumphed over death. In Jesus, God gives us eternal life, he gives it to everyone, and thanks to him everyone has the hope of a life even truer than this one. The life that God prepares for us is not a mere embellishment of the present one: it surpasses our imagination, for God continually amazes us with his love and with his mercy.

Therefore, what will happen is quite the opposite of what the Sadducees expected. It is not this life that will serve as a reference point for eternity, for the other life that awaits us; rather, it is eternity—that life—which illumines and gives hope to the earthly life of each one of us! If we look at things from only a human perspective, we tend to say that man's journey moves from life to death. This is what we see! But this is only so if we look at things from a human perspective. Jesus turns this perspective upside down and states that our pilgrimage goes from death to life: the fullness of life! We are on a journey, on a pilgrimage toward the fullness of life, and that fullness of life is what illumines our journey! Therefore death stands behind us, not before us.

....

We are on a journey, on a pilgrimage toward the fullness of life, and that fullness of life is what illumines our journey!

Before us is the God of the living, the God of the covenant, the God who bears my name, our names stand before us, as he said: "I am the God of Abraham, of Isaac, of Jacob," and also the God with my name, with your name . . . with our names. The God of the living! . . . Before us stands the final defeat of sin and death, the beginning of a new time of joy and of endless light. But already on this earth, in prayer, in the Sacraments, in fraternity, we encounter Jesus and his love, and thus we may already taste something of the risen life. The experience we have of his love and his faithfulness ignites in our hearts like a fire and increases our faith in the resurrection. In fact, if God is faithful and loves, he cannot be thus for only a limited time: faithfulness is eternal, it cannot change. God's love is eternal, it cannot change! It is not only for a time: it is forever! It is for going forward! He is faithful forever and he is waiting for us, each one of us, he accompanies each one of us with his eternal faithfulness.

Maria Teresa Bonzel, Foundress of the Poor Franciscan Sisters of Perpetual Adoration, who lived in the nineteenth century, will be beatified this afternoon in Paderborn, Germany. The Eucharist was the source from which she drew spiritual energy to dedicate herself with untiring charity to the weakest. Let us praise the Lord for her witness!

I wish to assure my closeness to the people of the Philippines and of that region. They have been hit by a tremendous typhoon. Unfortunately, there have been a great many victims and enormous damage. Let us pray for a moment, in silence, and then to Our Lady, for these brothers and sisters of ours, and let us try to also give them concrete help. Let us pray in silence.

Today is the seventy-fifth anniversary of the so-called "Crystal Night": the violence carried out on the night between November 9 and 10, 1938, against the Jews, their synagogues, their homes and stores marked a sad step toward the tragedy of the Shoah. Let us renew our closeness and solidarity to the Jewish people, to our elder brothers and sisters. And let us pray to God that the remembrance of the past, the remembrance of past sins, might help us to be always watchful against every form of hatred and intolerance.

This Sunday in Italy, the Day of Thanksgiving is celebrated. I join my voice with those of the bishops in expressing my closeness to the world of agriculture, especially to young people who have chosen to work the land. I encourage everyone to commit themselves to ensuring that no one will go without proper and adequate nourishment.

I greet all of the pilgrims who have come from various countries, the families, the parish groups, the associations . . .

I wish everyone a blessed Sunday. Goodbye and have a good lunch!

I CONFESS ONE BAPTISM

NOVEMBER 13, 2013

ST. PETER'S SQUARE

Dear Brothers and Sisters, good morning!

In the *Creed*, through which we make our Profession of Faith every Sunday, we state: "I confess one Baptism for the forgiveness of sins." It is the only explicit reference to a Sacrament contained in the *Creed*. Indeed, Baptism is the "door" of faith and of Christian life. The Risen Jesus left the Apostles with this charge: "Go into all the world and preach the Gospel to the whole of creation. He who believes and is baptized will be saved" (Mk 16:15-16). The Church's mission is to evangelize and remit sins through the Sacrament of Baptism. But let us return to the words of the *Creed*. The expression can be divided into three points: "*I confess*"; "*one Baptism*"; "*for the remission of sins*."

1. "*I profess.*" What does this mean? It is a solemn term that indicates the great importance of the object, that is, of Baptism. In fact, by pronouncing these words we affirm our true identity as children of God. Baptism is in a certain sense the identity card of the Christian, his birth certificate, and the act of his birth into the Church. All of you know the day on which you were born and you celebrate it as your birthday, don't you? We all celebrate our birthday. I ask you a question, that I have already asked several times, but I'll ask it again: who among you remembers the date of your Baptism? Raise your hands: they are few (and I am not asking the Bishops so as not to embarrass them . . .).

....

This is your homework: find out the day on which you were born to the Church, and give thanks to the Lord, because at Baptism he has opened the door of his Church to us.

Let's do something: today, when you go home, find out what day you were baptized, look for it, because this is your second birthday. The first birthday is the day you came into life and the second birthday is the one on which you came into the Church. Will you do this? This is your homework: find out the day on which you were born to the Church, and give thanks to the Lord, because at Baptism he has opened the door of his Church to us. At the same time, Baptism is tied to our faith in the remission of sins. The Sacrament of Penance or Confession is, in fact, like a "second baptism" that refers back always to the first to strengthen and renew it. In this sense, the day of our Baptism is the point of departure for this most beautiful journey, a journey toward God that lasts a lifetime, a journey of conversion that is continually sustained by the Sacrament of Penance. Think about this: when we go to confess our weaknesses, our sins, we go to ask the pardon of Jesus, but we also go to renew our Baptism through his forgiveness. And this is beautiful, it is like celebrating the day of Baptism in every Confession. Therefore, Confession is not a matter of sitting down in a torture chamber, rather it is a celebration. Confession is for the baptized! To keep clean the white garment of our Christian dignity!

2. The second element: "*one Baptism.*" This expression refers to that of St. Paul: "one Lord, one faith, one Baptism" (Eph 4:5). The word "Baptism" literally means "immersion," and in fact this Sacrament constitutes a true spiritual immersion in the death of Christ, from which one rises with Him like a new creation (cf. Rom 6:4). It is the washing of regeneration and of illumination. Regeneration because it actuates that birth by water and the Spirit without which no one may enter the Kingdom of Heaven (cf. Jn 3:5). Illumination because through Baptism the human person becomes filled with the grace

of Christ, "the true light that enlightens every man" (Jn 1:9) and dispels the shadows of sin. That is why in the ceremony of Baptism the parents are given a lit candle, to signify this illumination; Baptism illuminates us from within with the light of Jesus. In virtue of this gift the baptized are called to become themselves "light"—the light of the faith they have received—for their brothers, especially for those who are in darkness and see no glimmer of light on the horizon of their lives.

> **When we go to confess our weaknesses, our sins, we go to ask the pardon of Jesus, but we also go to renew our Baptism through his forgiveness.**

We can ask ourselves: is Baptism, for me, a fact of the past, relegated to a date, that date which you are going to go look for today, or is it a living reality, that pertains to my present, to every moment? Do you feel strong, with the strength that Christ gave you by his death and his Resurrection? Or do you feel low, without strength? Baptism gives strength and it gives light. Do you feel enlightened, with that light that comes from Christ? Are you a man or woman of light? Or are you a dark person, without the light of Jesus? We need to take the grace of Baptism, which is a gift, and become a light for all people!

3. Lastly, a brief mention of the third element: "*for the remission of sins.*" In the Sacrament of Baptism all sins are remitted, original sin and all of our personal sins, as well as the suffering of sin. With Baptism the door to an effectively new life is opened, one which is not burdened by the weight of a negative past, but rather already feels the beauty and the goodness of the Kingdom of Heaven. It is the powerful intervention of God's mercy in our lives, to save us. This saving intervention does not take away our human nature and its weakness—we are all weak and we are all sinners—and it does not take from us our responsibility to ask for forgiveness every time we err! I cannot be baptized many times, but I can go to Confession and by doing so renew the grace of Baptism. It is as though I were being baptized for a second time. The Lord Jesus is very very good and never tires of forgiving us. Even when the door that Baptism opens to us in order to enter the Church is a little closed, due to our weaknesses and our sins. Confession reopens it, precisely because it is a second Baptism that forgives us of everything and illuminates us to go forward with the light of the Lord. Let us go forward in this way, joyfully, because life should be lived with the joy of Jesus Christ; and this is a grace of the Lord.

I offer an affectionate greeting to all the English-speaking pilgrims and visitors present at today's Audience . . . May Jesus Christ confirm you in faith and make you witnesses of his love and mercy to all people. God bless you all!

Dear Brothers and Sisters,

I learned with great sorrow that two days ago in Damascus mortar rounds killed several children returning home from school as well as the school bus driver. Other children were left wounded. Please, these tragedies must never happen, ever! Let us pray intensely! In these days we are praying and joining forces to help our brothers and sisters in the Philippines, struck by a typhoon. These are the true battles to fight. For life! Never for death!

THE WAITING
PERIOD

NOVEMBER 17, 2013

ST. PETER'S SQUARE

Dear Brothers and Sisters, good morning!

This Sunday's Gospel passage (Lk 21:5-19) is the first
part of Jesus' discourse on the end times. He delivers it in
Jerusalem, close to the Temple, prompted by people dis-
cussing the Temple and its beauty. The Temple was very
beautiful. Jesus says: "As for these things which you see,
the days will come when there shall not be left here one
stone upon another" (Lk 21:6). Of course they asked him:
When will this happen? What will the signs be? But Jesus
moves the focus from these secondary aspects—i.e. when
will it be? What will it be like?—to the truly important
questions. Firstly, not to let oneself be fooled by false
prophets nor to be paralyzed by fear. Secondly, to live this

time of expectation as a time of witness and perseverance. We are in this time of waiting, in expectation of the coming of the Lord.

Jesus' words are perennially relevant, even for us today living in the twenty-first century too. He repeats to us: "Take heed that you are not led astray; for many will come in my name" (v. 8). This Christian virtue of understanding is a call to discern where the Lord is, and where the evil spirit is present. Today, too, in fact there are false "saviors" who attempt to replace Jesus: worldly leaders, religious gurus, even sorcerers, people who wish to attract hearts and minds to themselves, especially those of young people. Jesus warns us: "Do not follow them, do not follow them!"

The Lord also helps us not to be afraid in the face of war, revolution, natural disasters and epidemics. Jesus frees us from fatalism and false apocalyptic visions.

The second aspect challenges us as Christians and as a Church: Jesus predicts that his disciples will have to suffer painful trials and persecution for his sake. He reassures them, however, saying: "Not a hair of your head will perish" (v. 18). This reminds us that we are completely in God's hands! The trials we encounter for our faith and our commitment to the Gospel are occasions to give witness; we must not distance ourselves from the Lord, but instead abandon ourselves even more to him, to the power of his Spirit and his grace.

I am thinking at this moment, let everyone think together. Let us do so together: let us think about our many Christian brothers and sisters who are suffering persecution for their faith. There are so many. Perhaps more now than in past centuries. Jesus is with them. We too are united to them with our prayers and our love; we admire their courage and their witness. They are our brothers and sisters who, in many parts of the world, are suffering for their faithfulness to Jesus Christ. Let us greet them with heartfelt affection.

······································

Let us think about our many Christian brothers and sisters who are suffering persecution for their faith. There are so many. Perhaps more now than in past centuries. Jesus is with them.

At the end Jesus makes a promise which is a guarantee of victory: "By your endurance you will gain your lives" (v. 19). There is so much hope in these words! They are a call to hope and patience, to be able to wait for the certain fruits of salvation, trusting in the profound meaning of life and of history: the trials and difficulties are part of the bigger picture; the Lord, the Lord of history, leads all to fulfillment. Despite the turmoil and disasters that upset the world, God's design of goodness and mercy will be fulfilled! And this is our hope: go forward on this path, in God's plan which will be fulfilled. This is our hope.

Jesus' message causes us to reflect on our present time and gives us the strength to face it with courage and hope, with Mary who always accompanies us.

I greet all of you, families, associations and groups, who have come to Rome from other places in Italy and other parts of the world . . .

Today the Eritrean community of Rome is celebrating the Feast of St Michael. Let us warmly greet them!

Today is the World Day of Remembrance for Road Traffic Victims. I assure you of my prayers, and I encourage you to continue in your efforts to prevent accidents, because regulated prudence and compliance are the first steps to protecting yourselves and others.

Now I would like to recommend a medicine to you. Some of you may be wondering: "Is the Pope a pharmacist now?" It is a special medicine which will help you to benefit from the Year of Faith, as it soon will come to an end. It is a medicine that consists of fifty-nine threaded beads; a "spiritual medicine" called *Misericordin*. A small box containing fifty-nine beads on a string. This little box contains the medicine, and will be distributed to you by volunteers as you leave the Square. Take them! There is a rosary, with which you can pray the Chaplet of Divine

Mercy, spiritual help for our souls and for spreading love, forgiveness and brotherhood everywhere. Do not forget to take it, because it is good for you. It is good for the heart, the soul, and for life in general!

I wish you all a blessed Sunday. Goodbye and have a good lunch!

THE ECCLESIAL DIMENSION OF FORGIVENESS

NOVEMBER 20, 2013

ST. PETER'S SQUARE

Dear Brothers and Sisters, good morning!

Last Wednesday I spoke about the *remission of sins*, referred to in a special way at Baptism. Today let us continue on the theme of the remission of sins, but in reference to the "*power of the keys*," as it is called, which is a biblical symbol of the mission that Jesus entrusted to the Apostles.

First of all, we must remember that *the principal agent in the forgiveness of sins is the Holy Spirit*. In his first appearance to the Apostles, in the Upper Room, the Risen Jesus made the gesture of breathing on them saying: "Receive the Holy Spirit. If you forgive the sins of any, they are forgiven; if you retain the sins of any, they are retained" (Jn 20:22, 23). Jesus, transfigured in his body, is already the new man who offers the Paschal gifts, the fruit of his death and resurrection. What are these gifts? Peace, joy, the forgiveness of sins, mission, but above all he gives the Spirit who is the source of all these. The breath of Jesus, accompanied by the words with which he communicates the Spirit, signifies the transmission of life, the new life reborn from forgiveness.

The breath of Jesus, accompanied by the words with which he communicates the Spirit, signifies the transmission of life, the new life reborn from forgiveness.

But before making this gesture of breathing and transmitting the Holy Spirit, Jesus reveals the wounds in his hands and side: these wounds represent the price of our salvation. The Holy Spirit brings us God's pardon "by passing through" Jesus' wounds. These wounds he wished to keep; even now in Heaven he is showing the Father the wounds by which he redeemed us. By the power of these wounds, our sins are pardoned: thus, Jesus gave his life for our peace, for our joy, for the gift of grace in our souls, for the forgiveness of our sins. It is very very beautiful to look at Jesus in this way!

And we come to the second element: Jesus gave the Apostles the power to forgive sins. It is a little difficult to understand how a man can forgive sins, but Jesus gives this power. *The Church is the depository of the power of the keys*, of opening or closing to forgiveness. God forgives every man in his sovereign mercy, but he himself willed that those who belong to Christ and to the Church receive forgiveness by means of the ministers of the community. Through the apostolic ministry the mercy of God reaches me, my faults are forgiven and joy is bestowed on me. In this way Jesus calls us to live out reconciliation in the ecclesial, the community, dimension as well. And this is very beautiful. The Church, who is holy and at the same time in need of penitence, accompanies us on the journey of conversion throughout our life. The Church is not mistress of the power of the keys, but a servant of the ministry of mercy and rejoices every time she can offer this divine gift.

Perhaps many do not understand the ecclesial dimension of forgiveness, because individualism, subjectivism, always dominates, and even we Christians are affected by this. Certainly, God forgives every penitent sinner, personally, but the Christian is tied to Christ, and Christ is united to the Church. For us Christians there is a further gift, there is also a further duty: to pass humbly through the ecclesial community. We have to appreciate it; it is a gift, a cure, a protection as well as the assurance that God has forgiven me. I go to my brother priest and I say:

"Father, I did this. . . ." And he responds: "But I forgive you; God forgives you." At that moment, I am sure that God has forgiven me! And this is beautiful, this is having the surety that God forgives us always, he never tires of forgiving us. And we must never tire of going to ask for forgiveness. You may feel ashamed to tell your sins, but as our mothers and our grandmothers used to say, it is better to be red once than yellow a thousand times. We blush once but then our sins are forgiven and we go forward.

Lastly, a final point: *the priest is the instrument for the forgiveness of sins.* God's forgiveness is given to us in the Church, it is transmitted to us by means of the ministry of our brother, the priest; and he too is a man, who, like us in need of mercy, truly becomes the instrument of mercy, bestowing on us the boundless love of God the Father. Priests and bishops too have to go to confession: we are all sinners. Even the Pope confesses every fifteen days, because the Pope is also a sinner. And the confessor hears what I tell him, he counsels me and forgives me, because we are all in need of this forgiveness. Sometimes you hear someone claiming to confess directly to God . . . Yes, as I said before, God is always listening, but in the Sacrament of Reconciliation he sends a brother to bestow his pardon, the certainty of forgiveness, in the name of the Church.

The service that the priest assumes a ministry, on behalf of God, to forgive sins is very delicate and requires that his heart be at peace, that the priest have peace in his heart; that he not mistreat the faithful, but that he be gentle, benevolent and merciful; that he know how to plant hope in hearts and, above all, that he be aware that the brother or sister who approaches the Sacrament of Reconciliation seeking forgiveness does so just as many people approached Jesus to be healed. The priest who is not of this disposition of mind had better not administer this sacrament until he has addressed it. The penitent faithful have the right, all faithful have the right, to find in priests servants of the forgiveness of God.

Dear brothers, as members of the Church are we conscious of the beauty of this gift that God himself offers us? Do we feel the joy of this cure, of this motherly attention that the Church has for us? Do we know how to appreciate it with simplicity and diligence? Let us not forget that God never tires of forgiving us; through the ministry of priests he holds us close in a new embrace and regenerates us and allows us to rise again and resume the journey. For this is our life: to rise again continuously and to resume our journey.

Tomorrow, November 21, is the liturgical memorial of the Presentation of Mary Most Holy in the Temple, we will celebrate the Day *pro Orantibus*, dedicated to the cloistered religious communities. It is an opportune occasion to thank the Lord for the gift of so many people who, in monasteries and hermitages, dedicate themselves to

God in prayer and in silent work. Let us give thanks to the Lord for their witness of cloistered life and let us not fail to provide spiritual and material support to these our brothers and sisters, so that they may fulfil their important mission.

On November 22 the United Nations will inaugurate the *International Year of Family Farming*, meant to underline that the farming economy and rural development find in the family workers who are respectful of creation and attentive to concrete necessities. Also in work, the family is a model of brotherhood in living out the experience of unity and solidarity among all its members, with a greater sensibility for those who are most in need of care and help, by preventing the outcrop of possible social conflicts. For these reasons, as I express my satisfaction at such a timely initiative, I hope that it may contribute to a clearer appreciation of the innumerable benefits that the family brings to economic, social, cultural and moral growth of the entire human community.

I offer an affectionate greeting to all the English-speaking pilgrims and visitors present at today's Audience . . . Upon all of you, I invoke God's blessings of peace and joy!

Lastly, my affectionate thoughts turn to *young people*, to the *sick* and to *newlyweds*. In the month of November the liturgy invites us to pray for the departed. Let us not forget our loved ones, our benefactors and all those who have preceded us in the faith: the Eucharistic Celebration is the best spiritual help that we can offer to their souls, especially those who are most abandoned. And in this moment we cannot but recall the victims of recent floods in Sardinia: Let us pray for them and for they families and let us stand in solidarity with those who have suffered damage. Let us now say a little prayer in silence and then let us pray to Our Lady that she bless and help all our Sardinian brothers and sisters. And now let us pray in silence (. . .) *Hail Mary* . . .

SOLEMNITY OF OUR LORD JESUS CHRIST, KING OF THE UNIVERSE

NOVEMBER 24, 2013

ST. PETER'S SQUARE

Before concluding this celebration, I would like to greet all the pilgrims, families, parish groups, associations and movements, who have come from many countries. . . . I greet the Ukrainian community, which is commemorating the eightieth anniversary of the *Holodomor*, the "great famine" brought on by the Soviet Regime and resulting in millions of victims.

Today our grateful thoughts turn to missionaries who, over the course of centuries, have proclaimed the Gospel and spread the seed of faith to many parts of the world;

among these Bl. Junípero Serra, the Spanish Franciscan missionary. Today marks the third centenary of his birth.

I do not want to finish without addressing a thought to all those who have worked to carry forward this Year of Faith. Archbishop Rino Fisichella, who has led this journey: I thank him deeply from my heart, he and all of his collaborators. Thank you very much!

Now let us pray the Angelus together. With this prayer we invoke the protection of Mary especially for our brothers and sisters who are being persecuted for their faith, and they are many! . . .

I thank you all for your presence at this Concelebration. I wish you a good Sunday and a good lunch.

TO DIE IN CHRIST

NOVEMBER 27, 2013

ST. PETER'S SQUARE

Dear Brothers and Sisters,

Good morning, and compliments on your courage in coming out to the Square in this cold. Many compliments.

I wish to complete the catechesis on the *Creed* delivered during the Year of Faith, which concluded last Sunday. In this catechesis and in the next, I would like to consider the subject of the resurrection of the body, by seeking to grasp a deeper understanding of two of its aspects as they are presented in the *Catechism of the Catholic Church*; i.e. our dying and our rising in Jesus Christ. Today I shall consider the first aspect, "dying in Christ."

1. Among us there is commonly *a mistaken way of looking at death*. Death affects us all, and it questions us in a profound way, especially when it touches us closely, or when it takes the little ones, the defenseless in such a

way that it seems "scandalous." I have always been struck by the question: why do children suffer? why do children die? If it is understood as the end of everything, death frightens us, it terrifies us, it becomes a threat that shatters every dream, every promise, it severs every relationship and interrupts every journey. This happens when we consider our lives as a span of time between two poles: birth and death; when we fail to believe in a horizon that extends beyond that of the present life; when we live as though God did not exist. This concept of death is typical of atheistic thought, which interprets life as a random existence in the world and as a journey toward nothingness. But there is also a practical atheism, which consists in living for one's own interests alone and living only for earthly things. If we give ourselves over to this mistaken vision of death, we have no other choice than to conceal death, to deny it, or to trivialize it so that it does not make us afraid.

2. However, the "heart" of man, with its desire for the infinite, which we all have, its longing for eternity, which we all have, rebels against this false solution. And so what is the *Christian meaning of death*? If we look at the most painful moments of our lives, when we have lost a loved one—our parents, a brother, a sister, a spouse, a child, a friend—we realize that even amid the tragedy of loss, even when torn by separation, the conviction arises in the heart that everything cannot be over, that the good given and received has not been pointless. There is

a powerful instinct within us which tells us that our lives do not end with death.

This thirst for life found its true and reliable answer in the Resurrection of Jesus Christ. Jesus' Resurrection does not only give us the certainty of life after death, it also illumines the very mystery of the death of each one of us. If we live united to Jesus, faithful to him, we will also be able to face the passage of death with hope and serenity. In fact, the Church prays: "If the certainty of having to die saddens us, the promise of future immortality consoles us." This is a beautiful prayer of the Church! A person tends to die as he has lived. If my life has been a journey with the Lord, a journey of trust in his immense mercy, I will be prepared to accept the final moment of my earthly life as the definitive, confident abandonment into his welcoming hands, awaiting the face to face contemplation of his Face. This is the most beautiful thing that can happen to us: to contemplate face to face the marvellous countenance of the Lord, to see Him as he is, beautiful, full of light, full of love, full of tenderness. This is our point of arrival: to see the Lord.

> **Jesus' Resurrection does not only give us the certainty of life after death, it also illumines the very mystery of the death of each one of us.**

3. Against this horizon we understand Jesus' invitation to be ever ready, watchful, knowing that life in this world is given to us also in order to prepare us for the afterlife, for life with the heavenly Father. And for this there is a sure path: *preparing oneself well for death*, staying close to Jesus. This is surety: I prepare myself for death by staying close to Jesus. And how do we stay close to Jesus? Through prayer, in the Sacraments and also in the exercise of charity. Let us remember that he is present in the weakest and the most needy. He identified himself with them, in the well known parable of the Last Judgment, in which he says: "for I was hungry and you gave me food, I was thirsty and you gave me drink, I was a stranger and you welcomed me, I was naked and you clothed me, I was sick and you visited me, I was in prison and you came to me . . . 'as you did it to one of the least of these my brethren, you did it to me'" (Mt 25:35-36, 40).

Therefore, a sure path comes by recovering the meaning of Christian charity and fraternal sharing, by caring for the bodily and spiritual wounds of our neighbor. Solidarity in sharing sorrow and infusing hope is a premise and condition for receiving as an inheritance that Kingdom which has been prepared for us. The one who practices mercy does not fear death. Think well on this: the one who practices mercy does not fear death! Do you agree? Shall we say it together so as not to forget it? The one who practices mercy does not fear death. And why does he not fear it? Because he looks death in the face in the wounds of his brothers and sisters, and he overcomes it with the love of Jesus Christ.

If we will open the door of our lives and hearts to our littlest brothers and sisters, then even our own death will become a door that introduces us to heaven, to the blessed homeland, toward which we are directed, longing to dwell forever with God our Father, with Jesus, with Our Lady and with the Saints.

I greet all the English-speaking pilgrims present at today's Audience . . . Upon you and your families I invoke God's blessings of joy and peace! Lastly, my affectionate thoughts turn to *young people*, the *sick* and *newlyweds*. This Sunday we will begin the liturgical season of Advent. Dear *young people*, prepare your hearts to receive Jesus the Savior; dear *sick people*, offer up your suffering that others may recognize Christmas as Christ's encounter with frail human nature; and you, dear *newlyweds*, live out your marriage as a reflection of God's love in your personal history.

THE HORIZON OF HOPE

DECEMBER 1, 2013

ST. PETER'S SQUARE

Dear Brothers and Sisters, good morning!

Today, on the First Sunday of Advent, we begin a new liturgical year; that is, *a new journey of the People of God* with Jesus Christ, our Shepherd, who guides us through history toward the fulfillment of the Kingdom of God. Therefore, this day has a special charm, it makes us experience deeply the meaning of history. We rediscover the beauty of all being on a journey: the Church, with her vocation and mission, and all humanity, peoples, civilizations, cultures, all on a journey across the paths of time.

But where are we journeying? Is there a common goal? And what is this goal? The Lord responds to us through the prophet Isaiah, saying: "It shall come to pass in the latter days that the mountain of the house of the Lord shall be established as the highest of the mountains, and shall be raised above the hills; and all the nations shall flow to it, and many peoples shall come, and say: 'Come, let us go up to the mountain of the Lord, to the house of the God of Jacob; that he may teach us his ways and that we may walk in his paths'" (2:2-3). This is what Isaiah says regarding the goal toward which we are travelling. It is *a universal pilgrimage toward a common goal*, which in the Old Testament is Jerusalem, where the Temple of the Lord rises. For from there, from Jerusalem came the revelation of the Face of God and of his Law. Revelation found its fulfillment in *Jesus Christ*, and he, the Word made flesh, became the "Temple of the Lord": he is both guide and goal of our pilgrimage, of the pilgrimage of the entire People of God; and in his light the other peoples may also walk toward the Kingdom of justice, toward the Kingdom of peace. The Prophet continues: "They shall beat their swords into plowshares, and their spears into pruning hooks; nation shall not lift up sword against nation, neither shall they learn war any more" (2:4). Allow me to repeat what the Prophet says; listen carefully: "They shall beat their swords into plowshares, and their spears into pruning hooks; nation shall not lift up sword against nation, neither shall they learn war any more." But when will this occur? What a beautiful day it shall be, when weapons are dismantled in order to be transformed into tools for work! What a beautiful day that shall be! And this is possible! Let us bet on hope, on the hope for peace, and it will be possible!

This journey never comes to an end. Just as in each of our lives we always need to begin again, to get up again, to rediscover the meaning of the goal of our lives, so also for the great human family it is always necessary to rediscover the common horizon toward which we are journeying. *The horizon of hope!* This is the horizon that makes for a good journey. The season of Advent, which we begin again today, restores this horizon of hope, a hope which does not disappoint for it is founded on God's Word. A hope which does not disappoint, simply because the

....

What a beautiful day it shall be, when weapons are dismantled in order to be transformed into tools for work! What a beautiful day that shall be!

Lord never disappoints! He is faithful! He does not disappoint! Let us think about and feel this beauty.

The model of this spiritual disposition, of this way of being and journeying in life, is the Virgin Mary. A simple girl from the country who carries within her heart the fullness of hope in God! In her womb, God's hope took flesh, it became man, it became history: Jesus Christ. Her *Magnificat* is the canticle of the People of God on a journey, and of all men and women who hope in God and in the power of his mercy. Let us allow ourselves to be guided by her, she who is mother, a mamma and knows how to guide us. Let us allow ourselves to be guided by her during this season of active waiting and watchfulness.

Dear brothers and sisters, today is the World Day for the battle against HIV/AIDS. We express our closeness to all people whom it has affected, especially children. This closeness is made concrete through the silent commitment of so many missionaries and workers. Let us pray for everyone, also for the doctors and those involved in research. May every sick person, without exception, have access to the care they need.

With affection I greet all the pilgrims here present: the families, parishes, associations.

I wish everyone a blessed beginning of Advent. Have a good lunch and goodbye.

I BELIEVE IN THE RESURRECTION OF THE BODY

DECEMBER 4, 2013

ST. PETER'S SQUARE

Dear Brothers and Sisters, good morning!

Today I wish to return to the affirmation "I believe in the resurrection of the body." This is not a simple truth and it is anything but obvious; living immersed in this world it is not easy for us to fathom a future reality. But the Gospel enlightens us: our resurrection is strictly bound to Jesus' Resurrection. The fact that he is risen is the proof that there is a resurrection of the dead. I would like to present several aspects regarding the relation between the Resurrection of Christ and our resurrection. He is risen, and because he rose, we too will be raised.

85

First, Sacred Scripture itself contains *a path toward full faith in the resurrection of the dead.* This is expressed as faith in God as creator of the whole man, soul and body, and as faith in God the Liberator, the God who is faithful to the covenant with his people. The Prophet Ezekiel, in a vision, contemplates the graves of the exiled which are are reopened and whose dry bones come back to life thanks to the breath of a living spirit. This vision expresses hope in the future "resurrection of Israel," that is, the rebirth of a people defeated and humiliated (cf. Ez 37:1-14).

Jesus, in the New Testament, brings to fulfilment this revelation, and ties faith in the resurrection to his own person and says: "I am the resurrection and the life" (Jn 11:25). It will be our Lord Jesus who on the last day raises those who have believed in him. Jesus has come among us, he became man like us in all things, except sin; in this way he took us with him on his return journey to the Father. He, the Word Incarnate, who died for us and rose again, gives to his disciples the Holy Spirit as a pledge of full communion in his glorious Kingdom, which we vigilantly await. This waiting is the source and reason for our hope: a hope that, if cultivated and guarded—our hope, if we cultivate and guard it—becomes a light that illumines our common history. Let us remember it always: we are disciples of the One who came, who comes every-day and who will come at the end. If we can manage to be more aware of this reality, we will be less fatigued by daily life, less prisoners of the ephemeral and more disposed to walk with a merciful heart on the way of salvation.

Another aspect: *What does it mean to rise again?* The resurrection of us all will take place on the last day, at the end of the world, through the omnipotence of God, who will return life to our bodies by reuniting them to our souls, through the power of Jesus' Resurrection. This is the fundamental explanation: because Jesus rose we will rise; we have the hope of resurrection because he has opened to us the door of resurrection. And this transformation, this transfiguration of our bodies is prepared for in this life by our relationship with Jesus, in the Sacraments, especially in the Eucharist. We, who

Jesus has come among us, he became man like us in all things, except sin; in this way he took us with him on his return journey to the Father.

are nourished in this life by his Body and by his Blood shall rise again like him, with him and through him. As Jesus rose with his own body but did not return to this earthly life, so we will be raised again with our own bodies which will be transfigured into glorified bodies. This is not a lie! This is true. We believe that Jesus is Risen, that Jesus is living at this moment. But do you believe that Jesus is alive? And if Jesus is alive, do you think that he will let us die and not make us rise? No! He is waiting for us, and because He is risen, the power of his resurrection will raise us all.

A last element: *already in this life we have within us a participation in the Resurrection of Christ.* If it is true that Jesus will raise us at the end of time, it is also true that, in a certain way, with him we have already risen. Eternal life has already begun in this moment, it begins during our lifetime, which is oriented to that moment of final resurrection. And we are already raised, in fact, through Baptism; we are inserted in the death and resurrection of Christ and we participate in the new life, in his life. Therefore, as we await the last day, we have within us a seed of resurrection, as an anticipation of the full resurrection which we shall receive as an inheritance. For this reason too, the body of each one of us is an echo of eternity, thus it should always be respected; and in particular, the life of those who suffer should be respected and loved, that they may feel the closeness of the Kingdom of God, of that state of eternal life toward which we are journeying. This thought gives us hope: we are walking toward the resurrection. To see Jesus, to encounter Jesus: this is our joy! We will all be together—not here in the Square, or elsewhere—joyful with Jesus. This is our destiny!

I offer an affectionate greeting to all the English-speaking pilgrims and visitors present at today's Audience . . . Upon you and your families I invoke God's blessings of joy and peace! I extend an affectionate thought to *young people*, the *sick* and *newlyweds*. Yesterday we celebrated the memorial of St. Francis Xavier, Patron of Missionaries. This holy priest reminds us of the duty of each to proclaim the Gospel. Dear *young people*, be courageous witnesses of your faith; dear *sick people*, offer your daily cross for the conversion of those far from the light of the Gospel; and you, dear *newlyweds*, be proclaimers of the love of Christ beginning in your family.

Now, I invite everyone to pray for the Greek-Orthodox nuns of St. Tecla in Maaloula, Syria, who were taken by force two days ago by armed men. Let us pray for these religious, for these sisters, and for all people who have been sequestered because of this ongoing conflict. Let us continue to pray and to work together for peace. Let us pray to Our Lady. *Hail Mary* . . .